Vermont
Facts and Symbols

by Kathy Feeney

Consultant:
Gainor B. Davis, Ph.D.
Director
Vermont Historical Society

Capstone press
Mankato, Minnesota

Capstone Press
151 Good Counsel Drive, P.O. Box 669, Mankato, Minnesota 56002
http://www.capstone-press.com

Library of Congress Cataloging-in-Publication Data
Feeney, Kathy, 1954–
    Vermont facts and symbols/by Kathy Feeney.—Rev. and updated ed.
    p. cm.—(The states and their symbols)
    Includes bibliographical references (p. 23) and index.
    Summary: Presents information about the state of Vermont, its nickname, motto, and emblems.
    ISBN 0-7368-2275-5 (hardcover)
    1. Emblems, State—Vermont—Juvenile literature. [1. Emblems, State—Vermont. 2. Vermont.] I. Title. II. Series.
CR203.V5 F44 2003
974.3—dc21   2002154899

Editorial Credits
Christianne C. Jones, update editor; Karen L. Daas, editor; Linda Clavel, production designer and illustrator; Alta Schaffer, update photo researcher; Heidi Schoof and Kimberly Danger, photo researchers

Photo Credits
GeoIMAGERY/Kay Shai, 22 (top)
The Image Finders/Rob Curtis/The Early Birder, cover
James P. Rowan, 22 (middle)
KAC Productions/Kathy Adams Clark, 20
One Mile Up, Inc., 8, 10 (inset)
Robert McCaw, 16
Unicorn Stock Photos/Marshall Prescott, 6; Andre Jenny, 10; Jean Higgins, 18
Vermont Travel Division, 14
Visuals Unlimited/Rob Simpson, 12; John D. Cunningham, 22 (bottom)

1 2 3 4 5 6 08 07 06 05 04 03

Table of Contents

Quebec

VERMONT

● **Burlington**　　**St. Johnsbury**

Montpelier ✪

▲ **Morgan**
🏛 **Horse Farm**

New York

🏛 **Green Mountain**
🏛 **National Forest**

Green Mountains

Connecticut River

New Hampshire

🏛 **Green Mountain**
🏛 **National Forest**

🏛 **Bennington**
🏛 **Battle Monument**

Massachusetts

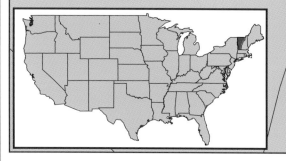

✪	**Capital**
○	**City**
▲	**Mountains**
🏛	**Places to Visit**
〰	**River**

Fast Facts

Capital: Montpelier is the capital of Vermont.

Largest City: Burlington is the largest city in Vermont. More than 38,800 people live there.

Size: Vermont covers 9,615 square miles (24,903 square kilometers). It is the 6th smallest state.

Location: Vermont is in the northeastern United States. Vermont is part of the New England region.

Population: About 608,827 people live in Vermont (2000 U.S. Census Bureau).

Statehood: On March 4, 1791, Vermont became the 14th state to join the United States.

Natural Resources: Vermont's natural resources include granite, marble, slate, and talc.

Manufactured Goods: Vermont's workers make furniture, computers, ski equipment, and machine tools. They also produce cheese and ice cream.

Crops: Vermont's farmers grow maple and apple trees, corn, and hay. They also raise dairy cattle.

In the 1600s, French explorers traveled near what is now Vermont. They named the mountains they saw "les monts verts," or the Green Mountains. State officials adopted the name Vermont in 1777. This name refers to the Green Mountains. Vermont's nickname, the Green Mountain State, also comes from this mountain range.

The Green Mountains are part of the Appalachians. The Green Mountains extend from north to south through the center of Vermont. Birch, beech, and pine trees cover the mountains. Spruce and sugar maple trees also grow throughout the Green Mountains. These trees give the mountains their green color.

The Long Trail stretches through the Green Mountains. Hikers travel along this 260-mile (418-kilometer) trail that runs from Canada to southwestern Vermont.

The Green Mountains cover more than 353,757 acres (143,165 hectares).

State Seal and Motto

Vermont's government adopted its state seal in 1937. The seal represents Vermont's government. The seal also makes government papers official.

Ira Allen designed the state seal in 1779. The General Assembly began to use the seal in 1779. But Allen's design did not become the official seal until 1937.

The top half of Vermont's seal shows a landscape. Wheat bundles and a cow represent agriculture. The Green Mountains are at the top of the landscape.

A forest appears in the center of the seal. A pine tree in the center of the forest has 14 branches. Vermont was the 14th state to join the United States.

The state's name and motto appear at the bottom of the seal. Vermont's motto is "Freedom and Unity." Vermonters chose this motto because they wanted the freedom to make decisions for their state. They also wanted to be part of the United States.

Waves at the bottom of Vermont's seal represent water.

State Capitol and Flag

Montpelier is the capital of Vermont. Vermont's capitol building is in Montpelier. Government officials meet there to make the state's laws.

Vermont has had three capitols. Workers built the first capitol from wood in 1808. They built a larger capitol from brick and granite in 1833. Fire destroyed the second capitol in 1857.

Workers completed Vermont's current capitol in 1859. They made the building from white marble found in Vermont.

Vermont's capitol has a gold-covered dome. A figure of Ceres stands on top of the dome. Ceres is the Greek goddess of agriculture.

Vermont officials adopted the state flag in 1923. The flag has a blue background. The state coat of arms appears in the center of the flag. Vermont's motto is on a red scroll below the coat of arms.

Vermont architect Thomas Silloway designed the current state capitol.

State Bird

The hermit thrush became Vermont's state bird in 1941. Officials chose this songbird because it lives in all of the state's 14 counties.

Hermit thrushes are brown. They have dark brown spots on their neck and breast. Hermit thrushes have a dark brown bill. Their short tail is red-brown.

Hermit thrushes live in woodlands. They live in shrubs or on low tree branches. Hermit thrushes eat insects and berries found in woodlands.

The female hermit thrush builds a nest from grass, leaves, and weeds. She lays four to six eggs each spring. The eggs are blue-green with dark spots.

Hermit thrushes live in Vermont only when the weather is warm. They fly south to warmer places each fall. Hermit thrushes return to Vermont each spring.

Hermit thrushes live in shrubs or on low tree branches.

State Tree

The sugar maple became Vermont's state tree in 1949. The sugar maple is important to Vermont's economy. Sugar maple trees produce sap. People process this sap to make maple syrup. Vermont is the leading producer of maple syrup in the United States.

Native Americans taught early Vermont settlers how to collect the sweet sap from the maple tree. This process is called tapping. Vermonters tap maple trees in late winter and early spring. They boil the sap to make maple syrup or maple sugar.

Sugar maple leaves have five points. In fall, the sugar maple's green leaves change colors. They become orange, yellow, and red.

The silver bark on a young sugar maple is smooth. The bark becomes dark and rough as the tree grows older.

A sugar maple can grow to be more than 80 feet (24 meters) tall.

State Flower

Vermont government officials named the red clover the official state flower in 1895. Red clovers grow wild in Vermont's fields and meadows.

Red clovers are tall plants. They can grow to be 3 feet (91 centimeters) tall. Leaves grow on their long, hairy stems. The leaves divide into three-leaf clovers.

Red clovers are flowering plants. Their red-purple blossoms grow in clusters. Honeybees suck nectar from the blossoms.

Farmers grow crops of red clovers. They feed red clovers to farm animals. Red clovers also help improve a farm's soil. They act like food for the soil and help other plants grow.

Early pioneers made tea from red clovers. They believed red clovers could cure some illnesses. Some people still use red clovers as medicine today.

Red clovers have hairy stems.

State Animal

The Morgan horse became Vermont's state animal in 1961. It is the only horse breed that can be traced to one stallion. This stallion was named for his owner, Justin Morgan. The music teacher and his horse lived in Vermont more than 200 years ago.

Morgan horses weigh about 900 pounds (408 kilograms). These muscular animals can grow to be about 5 feet (1.5 meters) tall at the shoulders. They can live as long as 30 years.

Morgan horses can be black, brown, or gray. They have long, full tails and manes. Their coats are soft and shiny. Morgan horses sometimes have white markings on their faces and lower legs.

People raise Morgan horses for many purposes. People ride Morgan horses on long trails. Morgan horses jump, trot, and pull carriages in horse shows. They also compete in races.

Some Vermonters raise Morgan horses.

More State Symbols

State Beverage: Milk became Vermont's state beverage in 1983. Milk is Vermont's most important farm product. People make cheese and ice cream from Vermont milk.

State Butterfly: Officials adopted the monarch butterfly as Vermont's state butterfly in 1987. Monarchs have orange wings with black veins and black borders.

State Cold Water Fish: Vermont officials chose the brook trout as Vermont's official cold water fish in 1978. Brook trout are dark green or gray.

State Rocks: Granite, marble, and slate became Vermont's state rocks in 1992. Workers construct buildings from granite and marble. They make floors from slate. Workers used Vermont's state rocks to build Radio City Music Hall in New York City and the U.S. Capitol building in Washington, D.C.

Monarch butterflies have a wingspan of 3 to 5 inches (8 to 13 centimeters).

Places to Visit

Bennington Battle Monument

The Bennington Battle Monument is in Old Bennington. The monument honors Vermont soldiers who fought in the 1777 Revolutionary War Battle of Bennington. The 306-foot (93-meter) tall monument is made of stone. Visitors take an elevator to the top of the monument.

Green Mountain National Forest

Two areas along the ridge of the Green Mountains make up Green Mountain National Forest. These areas became a national forest in 1932. Visitors canoe, fish, hike, and bike in Green Mountain National Forest. During winter, they ski, go snowmobiling, and drive dogsleds.

Morgan Horse Farm

The Morgan Horse Farm is in Weybridge. This breeding farm is a national historic site. The farm has hilly pastures and woodlands. Visitors see Morgan horses. They also tour the stables and watch a video about the history of the horse.

Words to Know

agriculture (AG-ruh-kul-chur)—producing crops, raising livestock, and other farming activities

coat of arms (KOHT UHV ARMZ)—a shield or a picture of a shield that has a design on it; the design usually is the symbol for a family, city, state, or country.

economy (e-KON-uh-mee)—the way a country or state runs its business, trade, and spending

explorer (ex-SPLOR-ur)—a person who travels to a new place to discover what it is like

landscape (LAND-skape)—an area of land that can be seen from one place

stallion (STAL-yuhn)—an adult male horse

Read More

Foran, Jill. *Vermont.* A Guide to American States. Mankato, Minn.: Weigl Publishers, 2001.

Kummer, Patricia K. *Vermont.* One Nation. Mankato, Minn.: Capstone Press, 2003.

Pelta, Kathy. *Vermont.* Hello U.S.A. Minneapolis: Lerner Publications, 2002.

Schaffer, David. *Vermont.* States. Berkeley Heights, NJ: MyReportLinks.com Books, 2003.

Useful Addresses

Vermont Department of Tourism and Marketing
6 Baldwin Street, 4th Floor
Drawer 33
Montpelier, VT 05633-1301

Vermont Historical Society
109 State Street
Montpelier, VT 05609-0901

Internet Sites

Do you want to find out more about Vermont?
Let FactHound, our fact-finding hound dog, do the research for you.

Here's how:
1) Visit **http://www.facthound.com**
2) Type in the **BOOK ID** number:
   0736822755
3) Click on **FETCH IT**.

FactHound will fetch Internet sites picked by our editors just for you!

Index